BLOCKCHAIN TECHNOLOGY

The Essential Quick & Easy Blueprint
To Understand Blockchain Technology
And Conquer The Next Thriving Economy!
Get Your First Mover Advantage Now!

VICTOR FINCH

AUVA PRESS

© Copyright 2017 Victor Finch - All rights reserved.

In no way is it legal to reproduce, duplicate, or transmit any part of this document in either electronic means or in printed format. Recording of this publication is strictly prohibited and any storage of this document is not allowed unless with written permission from the publisher. All rights reserved.

The information provided herein is stated to be truthful and consistent, in that any liability, in terms of inattention or otherwise, by any usage or abuse of any policies, processes, or directions contained within is the solitary and utter responsibility of the recipient reader. Under no circumstances will any legal responsibility or blame be held against the publisher for any reparation, damages, or monetary loss due to the information herein, either directly or indirectly.

Respective authors own all copyrights not held by the publisher.

Legal Notice:

This book is copyright protected. This is only for personal use. You cannot amend, distribute, sell, use, quote or paraphrase any part or the content within this book without the consent of the author or copyright owner. Legal action will be pursued if this is breached.

Disclaimer Notice:

Please note the information contained within this document is for educational and entertainment purposes only. Every attempt has been made to provide accurate, up to date and reliable complete information. No warranties of any kind are expressed or implied. Readers acknowledge that the author is not engaging in the rendering of legal, financial, medical or professional advice.

By reading this document, the reader agrees that under no circumstances are we responsible for any losses, direct or indirect, which are incurred as a result of the use of information contained within this document, including, but not limited to, —errors, omissions, or inaccuracies.

Trademarks:

Auva Press and the Auva Press logo are trademarks or registered trademarks and may not be used without written permission. All other trademarks are the property of their respective owners. Auva Press is not associated with any product or vendor mentioned in this book.

To friendship and to my family,

who make my world more meaningful

Abstract

People have used—and continue to use—the phrase "Blockchain technology" to imply different things. I know this is quite mystifying. Have you been using the term Blockchain technology to refer to the Bitcoin technology or other cryptocurrency systems such as Ethereum or Litecoin? Or, have you been using the term to refer to smart contracts?

Well, the term Blockchain technology can be ubiquitous. When Blockchain technology was invented, the discussion around it focused mainly on cryptocurrency systems and, more precisely, the Bitcoin. However, over the past few years, the discussion has shifted more towards the fundamental components of the Blockchain itself as a distributed ledger for transactions.

As a result, the Blockchain technology is finding its applications in other cryptocurrency systems, smart contracts, loan recording, healthcare data management, elections management and even stock transfers.

In the recent past, several companies have raced to leverage Blockchain technology in order to develop new products and services. It is not a secret that new startup firms such as OpenBazaar, Zapchain and BitFury, have transitioned to Blockchain technology to compete in today's fast-paced, complex and ever-changing business environment.Nonetheless, other companies, too, are leveraging on the use of Blockchain technology. The incumbent companies have been responding to new entrants by capitalizing on Blockchain technology to provide cutting edge solutions to their clients. For instance, WordPress.com, Overstock.com, Microsoft and Reddit are companies that have started to accept Bitcoin as a payment method.

What exactly is Blockchain? More precisely, what are the Blockchain technology fundamentals that you should be acquainted with? This book will provide you with a complete overview of the Blockchain technology, details of how the transactions are handled in the Blockchain ecosystem, applications, challenges and future prospects of Blockchain.

Are you ready to be mind blown?

CONTENTS

Abstract 1

Chapter 1 Introduction 3

Chapter 2 The Eagle Eye View 19

Chapter 3 The Finer Details of Blockchain technology 33

Chapter 4 Consensus Mechanisms in Blockchain Technology 43

Chapter 5 Factors to consider in consensus mechanisms 47

Chapter 6 Challenges of the Blockchain Technology 57

Chapter 7 The Future of Blockchain Technology 67

Chapter 8 Legal Implications of Blockchain Technology 79

Chapter 9 Legal impacts of the Blockchain technology 83

CONCLUSION 87

ABOUT THE AUTHOR 89

Chapter 1

Introduction

Over the past 8 years, a major IT disruptive innovation that is colloquially referred to as Blockchain emerged. This technology promises to revolutionize the manner in which transactional data is stored, shared and used. The core of this disruptive technology is formed around the concept of the distributed ledger system.

In this system, a consensus ledger is stored and maintained on a distributed set of computers that are able to communicate with others on a network. I know you're asking, "How can the consensus ledger revolutionize transactional data storage and sharing?"

Let me use the example of a distributed database to illustrate the importance of a distributed consensus ledger. Imagine a spreadsheet file that has duplicated hundreds or even thousands of times across a distributed set of computers. If this file were to be regularly updated by different users on the network, then problems of seamless updates and additions of data to the ledger were likely to arise.

The conventional way for updating and sharing such a file is that you send the document to the recipient and ask them to make necessary updates. Before you can update it, you have to wait until you receive the updated copy from the recipient because the file remains locked as you cannot edit it while the other person is also updating it.

Now try to figure out if there are thousands of users, or even millions, who would like to access and edit the same spreadsheet file. The challenge of storage, sharing and updating the ledger becomes imminent. That is how conventional database systems work today. These systems have been built with the assumption that two or more users shouldn't be editing or working on the same file at the same time.

It is the same concept that underpins the way banks maintain account balances and transfers. During the transaction, a particular file is locked to prevent two or more users from accessing it simultaneously. That is what the Blockchain technology tries to solve.

Actually, the Blockchain technology tosses the model of the conventional ledger on its head.

You can figure out the Blockchain technology as some sort of Google Sheets—the Google version of a conventional spreadsheet software—or Google Docs. With Google Sheets, both parties can have access to the same spreadsheet file and update it simultaneously. In this case, the Google Sheet files act as a shared distributed ledger where several users on the network can access and modify the contents of the files.

When you begin to figure out how the network can regularly update the Google Sheet or the ledger for that matter, you will begin to appreciate the role of Blockchain technology in storage and maintenance of the transactional data.

The ledger can make it conceivable for the entire distributed network of computers to develop, evolve, and even keep track of the indisputable and incorruptible history of transactions. Until recently, this technology has found its wide use in cryptocurrency systems such as the Bitcoin, Ethereum or Litecoin.

The cryptocurrency systems, however, are just the first of the many possible applications of the Blockchain technology. Other applications of the Blockchain technology are in smart contracts management, value registry management, and value web-based management.

Let's begin with the biggest question of all— what is the Blockchain technology about? Let's dive in and explore the fundamental concepts of the Blockchain technology.

History of the Blockchain technology

Up to this date, there has been a growing conjecture over who actually invented the Blockchain technology as well as the first cryptocurrency system—the Bitcoin. Well, the developer of the Blockchain technology goes by the code name Satoshi Nakamoto. Up to date, no one really knows (or has interacted with) Satoshi Nakamoto.

It is widely believed that Satoshi Nakamoto doesn't exist but is a pseudo-name used by unknown persons who designed the first Bitcoin cryptocurrency and the Blockchain technology. In Cryptography Mailing List in November 2008, they published a paper about distributed peer-to-peer currency system.

No other technology has been the subject of such a passionate debate since the development of the first Blockchain technology. Although the Blockchain technology was originally built to monitor and secure the Bitcoin transactions, recent developments and applications of the system have surpassed the distributed digital monetary transactions.

When the Bitcoin system was first released in 2009, there were major doubts and suppositions about the cryptocurrency's lack of security safeguards. The general speculations and doubts for the cryptocurrency, as well as the Blockchain ledger, prevented the currency system from being accepted as a digital currency. However, that impression has changed.

Today, several companies have come to accept the bitcoin as a method of payment because of cryptographic security protocols that are tamper-proof and guarantee the security of transactions on the network. Some of these companies are the Reddit, OverStock.com, PayPal, and Microsoft.

Actually, the Blockchain technology maintains a cryptographic record of each transaction that's made on the network. This makes it practically impossible to hack the system. For instance, if you were to hack the system successfully, you have to alter every single block of data in the entire Blockchain ecosystem.

As a result of rapid improvements in IT, the majority of people have begun to understand and appreciate the safeness of the Blockchain technology. Nevertheless, that's not all. Many companies have started to invest in Bitcoin to help save them money and accrue other benefits that the Blockchain technology brings in an organization.

In the recent past, several companies such as Zapchain, BitFury and OpenBazaar have raced to leverage Blockchain technology in order to develop new products and services for the ever fast-paced, complex and ever-changing business environment.

One of the major breakthroughs in the application of the Blockchain technology came in the year 2014 with smart contracts. Smart contracts provided users with the capabilities to customize and create their own Blockchain contracts, which involve monetary transactions and are trustworthy.

Simply put, smart contracts are essentially programs written to encode accurate conditions and outcomes that the parties involved can rely on and trust. In other words, the smart contract programs ensure a secure escrow service that's processed in real-time at zero marginal costs between participating parties.

If a transaction takes place between two or more parties, the smart contract program can actually verify if the product or the service has been sent by the supplier or not. A sum of money can be transmitted to the recipient only after the verification process has been completed by the smart contract program.

What about the Blockchain today?

The Blockchain technology has found its applications on several fronts. These areas include the insurance industry, loan recording in banks, healthcare data management, elections management and even stock transfers.

Some examples:

- OpenBazaar is doing ecommerce very differently with Blockchain technology. It is an open source free market that allows people to trade directly with each other without fees or restrictions.

- BitFury provides the expertise and opportunity for companies who are looking to digitize their assets and transact them securely over the internet.

How about Zapchain?

- Zapchain is a social media platform that leverages on Blockchain technology with a truly revolutionary idea in tipping to nurture high quality user engagement and content creation within its communities. It was once the darling and an upcoming promising start up.

However, it has announced its shut down in August 2016.

These new start up firms have transitioned to the use of Blockchain technology to compete in today's fast-paced, complex and ever-changing business environment. Nevertheless, there are challenges and hurdles that need to be overcome by the start up firms to survive in this very environment that there are competing to revolutionize with Blockchain technology.

The incumbent companies are responding to new entrants by capitalizing on Blockchain technology to provide cutting edge solutions to their clients. For example, the WordPress.com, the Overstock.com, Microsoft, and Reddit are companies that have started to accept Bitcoin as a payment method.

There you have it. Next, let's explore some of the revolutionary aspects of the Blockchain technology.

The Revolution of Blockchain technology

I cannot predict what the future holds for the Blockchain technology since I'm not a futurist. I also believe that the future is something that can be predicted with certainties. However, one thing is sure— the Blockchain technology is likely to have a significant bearing on the future of the world economy.

Several companies, traditionally against the use of this technology, have now begun to embrace it. In 2016, the Bank of England and the Bank of Canada—examples of companies that have been against the Blockchain and Bitcoin due to non-regulatory aspects— have expressed interest in the use of Blockchain technology because of the promising benefits of central banking.

In fact, because of the cost-cutting potential that the technology promises in the FinTech industry, several companies are betting on Blockchain technology to save billions of money through transparency, security, and accuracy.

If the Blockchain technology is promising several benefits to central banks, how will it impact peer-to-peer transactions—the hallmarks of the financial technology? Better still, does the Blockchain technology herald the starting of a new epoch when there will be no need for third party financial intermediaries?

The answer is yes.

It is a fact that the distributed financial ledger has capabilities of streamlining the inefficiencies in the financial transactional settlement and thereby disrupts the conventional business environment. Besides, the Blockchain technology provides alternative ways to ensure the security of transactions in all categories—especially the peer-to-peer transactions—which have already begun to take shape.

But how will the disruption occur?

Let's sample the financial services industry. The financial services industry is already undergoing serious disruption thanks to the Blockchain technology. Whether you call it transformation or innovation, it all boils down to the disruptive nature of the Blockchain technology. The financial services industry moves money, stores money, lends money, and trades in money and so on.

Every function of financial services industry is challenged by the Blockchain technology. For example, if it were implemented, the Blockchain technology could have serious implications on the MPESA—mobile phone-based money transfer system launched in Kenya by Safaricom—with regard to the movement and storage of money, a lending process in the network.

But it's not just the FinTech industry that is likely to be disrupted. Several startup and incumbent companies out there are working out modalities of leveraging the technology for many applications.

Some of these companies are:

- Storj. Storj is a decentralized distributed file storage system, which is trying to eliminate the costs that are being incurred in centralized databases such as One Drive and DropBox.
- NASDAQ. This is a US listed stock exchange company which is planning to transition to "proxy voting" by leveraging on Blockchain technology.
- Onename. This is a decentralized distributed identity storage network, which is trying to use the Blockchain technology to provide an alternative to the less-safe database storage capabilities.
- Modum. Modum is a Blockchain-based organization that is striving to ensure drug safety by leveraging on Blockchain technology to ensure immutability and public accessibility in the pharmaceutical supply chain.

And that, folks, is why the Blockchain technology is revolutionizing and changing the way the world does business.

Next, we will explore the basics of the Blockchain technology.

What is Blockchain?

A Blockchain—initially known as Block chain— is simply a distributed ledger of records. Think of a ledger as some kind of a book that facilitates the transfer of journal entries in a chronological order of a particular type. For instance, a ledger could store information about assets of an organization such as the Cash, the Accounts Receivable, the Inventory, the Investments and even equipment.

However, that's a conventional ledger.

Unlike the conventional ledger, which is important to note, the Blockchain has electronic data arranged in references or batches called *blocks* hence the name Blockchain. These blocks use cryptographic validation techniques to link themselves together and form a continuous database structure. Each block identifies the previous one using a hashing function.

I know you are thinking, "What are these cryptographic techniques?"

Well, cryptographic techniques are protocols that scramble or encrypt data exchanged in the Blockchain ecosystem to ensure that nobody tampers with the transactions or records. These protocols ensure that old transactions are maintained or stored forever while the new ones are added to the ledger irrevocably—a transaction can never be reversed once it has been recorded.

In fact, all users on the Blockchain network will view the same transaction history. The Blockchain is also distributed, which means that the ledger is not stored in a centralized location. It is also not managed by a particular person or persons. Instead, the ledger exists on multiple computers where it can be accessed and updated by multiple users simultaneously.

In a nutshell, the Blockchain can be viewed as an independent, immutable, and permanent database that coexists in multiple locations or servers which are shared by a community. So, who owns Blockchain? Can it be shut down?

Strictly speaking, no one owns the Blockchain technology, just like no one owns the internet. It's an open source technology where the ledger is stored on multiple computers (people volunteer their computers to be used as servers or nodes). Every node on the network, which is commonly referred to as miner, has a copy of the Blockchain. Every time a transaction takes place, the miners get notified and update themselves.

The process of adding and verifying transactions to the Blockchain is called mining. Now, every time a user successfully adds a transaction on the Blockchain and all the miners verify it, the user is rewarded with some incentives. For instance, for every successful addition and verification of a transaction in Bitcoin network, a reward of 25 bitcoins is given to the user.

Is Blockchain technology secure?

That is a good question.

No one owns the Blockchain technology. It isn't owned by a person, organization, or an entity. Therefore, each user or organization can view or access the status of Blockchain transaction at any given point in time; the system is becoming increasingly used to launch several applications ranging from cryptocurrencies to value registry management.

Being a revolutionary and disruptive technology, the security, and verifiability of transaction and transfer of data is achieved using complex mathematical cryptographic protocols—the public key cryptography. The nodes on the network form a validated consensus system where all the transactions that are added to the block must be confirmed and verified.

Because of its decentralized approach to management of transactions and use of public key cryptography, the system is resilient to network attacks. The distributed consensus algorithms that are used in the Blockchain technology render the system to be practically impossible to hack; hackers would require a high computational hashing power and hi-tech solutions to break it.

In fact, trust and transparency are two properties that make the Blockchain technology to be one of the most secure systems, which companies can rely upon. But this doesn't mean the system is full-proof secure. The system may be vulnerable to attacks, which can complicate the crux of its existence.

Thus, it's important for Blockchain developers to ensure they have put up concrete cyber security policies, controls, and measures for safety and integrity of the Blockchain transactions. With the continued development of the quantum computing—which will result in faster computers—it may not be the case. Other security concerns may arise.

For example, in the future, it might be possible to trace the node's identity from the Blockchain transactions or even through a node that has the permissions to decrypt the data. However, there have been very few reported cases of break-ins, so you can trust the technology.

What's next? In the next subtopic, we will explore the big picture of the Blockchain technology including how it works and how transactions are processed.

Chapter 2

The Eagle Eye View

Okay, so now that you have an idea about the Blockchain technology, how does it really work? More fundamentally, how are transactions processed in the Blockchain ecosystem?

Let's dive into some of the finer details about the Blockchain technology.

How Blockchain works

The most widely known and discoursed application of the Blockchain technology is the Bitcoin. Let's use the Bitcoin technology to illustrate how the Blockchain technology works.

A bitcoin is a digital currency. This means it can be used during the exchange of products and services, just like the US Dollar (USD), the Euro (EUR), the Chinese Yuan (CNY), and other currencies. One bitcoin is a solitary component of the Bitcoin digital currency. But just like the USD, it has no value.

It only attains a value once everybody agrees to trade goods and services in exchange for larger amounts of the currency that's under our regulation. In addition, we must believe that other users will do the same.

Now, to keep track of the volume of bitcoins that each of us owns in the Bitcoin ecosystem, the Blockchain uses a distributed ledger, a digital file that stores all the bitcoin transactions on the network.

As we have mentioned earlier, the ledger file—in this case the Blockchain— is not stored on a central server. In a normal currency system, the ledger will be maintained in a bank or a single data center. However, in the case of the Blockchain technology, the ledger will be distributed among several private computers across the world. These computers will be storing the data and executing the computations (transactions).

Each of the private computers in the Blockchain ecosystem will be called a node or a miner. Each node has a copy of the ledger file. For instance, if you wish to send 50 bitcoins to your friend—say, Bob—then you have to broadcast a message to all the network nodes indicating that you wish to send 50 bitcoins to Bob. This means your account balance will reduce by 50 bitcoins, while Bob's account balance will increase by 50 bitcoins.

Each node in the Blockchain network receives the broadcasted message and applies the requested transaction to their stored copy of the ledger. Both of your account balances will be updated across all the nodes on the Blockchain network. Having said that, what do you need to perform a Blockchain transaction?

Well, to perform transactions in the Blockchain ecosystem, all you need is a wallet. Think of a wallet as some kind of program—a software that you install on your computer—to enable you to exchange your bitcoins. As it is only you that should spend your money, your wallet is protected by special cryptographic techniques, which use different and connected keys.

Technically speaking, the cryptographic technique used to exchange the bitcoins in the Blockchain network is the public key cryptographic system. In this system, two keys are used to scramble the message: the private key and the public key. As you broadcast the message to the networked nodes, you will request Bob's public key (the public key is known to all the network nodes) and use it to scramble the broadcast message.

Simply put, the broadcast message is scrambled with a particular public key. Only the owner of the paired private key (Bob) will be able to decrypt and read the contents of the message. Now, Bob will now use his private key (the private key is only known to Bob) to de-scramble the message. In other words, when you encrypt the broadcast message with your own private key, then it is only the paired public key that can be used to decrypt it. Every node in the network must cross-check and validate that the transaction which has been requested is actually coming from you by decrypting the transacted broadcast message with the public key of your wallet. Interesting, isn't it?

Now, whenever you're encrypting the transaction request with your own wallet's private key, what you're actually undertaking is generating a digital signature which will be used by Blockchain computers to verify and validate the source and the legitimacy of the transaction. Think of a digital signature as a string of characters that combines your transaction request and your private key.

The digital signature cannot be used for other transactions. If you happen to change even a single character in the transaction, then the signature changes. This means that the transaction has been tampered with and all the nodes will be notified. Therefore, it is almost impossible to hack the Blockchain network.

It is important to note that your wallet's public keys will be known to all the nodes in the Blockchain network. Therefore, to send 50 bitcoins to Bob, you have to prove that you have the private key (which creates the digital signature) of the wallet since you will need to encrypt the broadcasted transaction message. The private key must never be revealed to anyone else in the network.

Each miner in the Blockchain network keeps a copy of the distributed ledger. How can you determine the amount of bitcoin money in your account? Good question.

The Blockchain ecosystem does not store the account balances at all for any node. Rather, it stores only the transactions that have been requested on the network. To determine the amount of money in your account balance, you should analyze and cross-check all the transactions that have taken place on the whole network which is connected to your wallet.

How does account balance verification process occur?

Ideally, the account balances the verification process, if possible, because of the links that point to previous transactions related to your wallet. For instance, if you are sending 50 bitcoins to Bob, then you have to create a broadcast transaction request to all the nodes in the network. This transaction request contains links to previous incoming transactions where the total account balance equals or exceeds 50 bitcoins.

In Blockchain technology, these links are commonly called the "inputs." As a matter of fact, every time you reference the inputs in the transaction, those that are not considered valid will automatically reflect. This is done automatically in your wallet and it can be verified by any node in the Blockchain network.

How can the Blockchain system trust the input transactions and consider them valid?

The Blockchain network will check all the previous transactions related to your wallet by using references that have inputs pointing to your wallet account. All the records of unspent transactions will be stored by the Blockchain nodes. This helps to simplify the verification process. Because of this security check, it is not possible to double-spend a number of received bitcoins.

Remember that all the source code that performs the transactions in the Bitcoin system is open source. Anyone with a computer—with installed wallet and an internet connection—

can start a transaction. If there is an error in the source code that broadcasts the transaction message, then all the associated bitcoins will be forever lost! Too bad.

The system is distributed, so there will be no customer support or anyone that you can call to help restore your bitcoin transactions. As a rule of thumb, it is vital that you use the Bitcoins recommended and official Bitcoin wallet software and store your password credentials in a safe repository.

The Bitcoin system arranges the transactions by placing them together into groups or blocks. Every block has a definite number of transactions. The transactions also link to the previous block. Therefore, it is vital to note that the blocks are arranged in a time-related chain; hence the whole system—the Blockchain.

Transactions are placed in the same block only if they have taken place at the same time. Other transactions, which are not yet in the same block, are considered to be unconfirmed. Each miner can group the transactions together into a block and broadcast the same information to all the network nodes as a recommendation for what the block should look like next.

So, how does the system agree on what a block should look like?

For a transaction to be added to the Blockchain it must have answers to very complex mathematical problems—cryptographic algorithms—generated by created hash functions. The only way to provide answers to this complex algorithm is to conjecture a random number which, when combined with previous block content, produces a defined result agreed upon by all the network nodes.

Any node that solves such a complex cryptographic algorithm earns the right to place the block on the chain in the whole network!

But what happens if two nodes solve the cryptographic algorithm at the same time and place their blocks to the system at the same time?

If this happens, then both blocks will be broadcasted to the network and each miner builds on the block that it has first received. However, the Blockchain system demands that each node immediately creates a block on any of the longest available Blockchain. If there is vagueness about the last block, then each node adopts the longest chain as the only viable option.

But rarely the system reaches this point because of the low probability the blocks will be solved simultaneously. In fact, it is practically impossible for multiple blocks to be solved simultaneously over and over again. What this means is that transactions will get more and more secure as time elapses. Those transactions that have been included in the blocks confirmed in the past are regarded to be more secure than those blocks, which have been recently included.

As a block is only inserted in the chain every 10 minutes (on average), then waiting for about 40 minutes from the moment when the transaction is added to the block for the first time provides a high probability that the processed transaction is secure.

All right. Now that you understand how Blockchain technology works, let's explore the superiority of Blockchain technology.

The Superiority of the Blockchain Technology

It is a fact that governments, banks, and even the private sector have been disrupted by the ever-growing influence of the Blockchain technology. Besides being faster, more cost-effective, more secure, and more efficient, Blockchain technology is a big step forward.

Below are the reasons why the Blockchain technology is superior to others:

#1: Trust

The main reason why Blockchain technology is superior to centralized database management systems is that it provides user's trust in the global-wide decentralized and open source system. The fact that there is a low probability the blocks will be solved simultaneously makes the system trustworthy.

In essence, transactions conducted on the network on multiple blocks in a repeated fashion are nearly impossible. In fact, the transactions will get more and more secure as time elapses. Already confirmed transactions, that have been included in the blocks in the past, are more secure than the blocks created recently. As a result of this feature, this system guarantees trusted communication among the Blockchain nodes.

#2: Innovation

With other cryptocurrency systems such as Ethereum and Litecoin invented on different protocols, there are always developers keen to improve on the existing protocol. In fact, if centralized networks were part of the privatized Blockchains, that would provide serious thoughts on how to make them robust and transparent.

This comes as a result of the synergy that is created by two technologies. In principle, private Blockchains will open all avenues for fresh ideas and innovation. You can think of the conventional database system as an "intranet." Now, the intranet on its own does not allow you to innovate and bring in fresh original ideas to your company.

But when you combine the intranet and the Internet— and that is what the Blockchain technology is providing—then you have a perfect mix of innovation and external options with massive amounts of control to your organization. In other words, you will be in a position to leverage the Blockchain technology to create other decentralized applications that are able to manage data efficiently and transfer value in a secure manner.

#3: You have complete control of all the transactions

If you apply the Blockchain technology in implementing the cryptocurrency systems, then you will be gaining complete control over transactions. Imagine a scenario where you have cash and you would like to spend it without involving a third party. In this scenario, you are not bothered about the bank charges and other levied charges when transacting goods and services.

Again, there will be no forms in case you want to give your cryptocurrency money to someone else. This is what you get with a Blockchain technology. When the technology is cascaded to other applications such as smart contracts, then you will begin to appreciate the level of control it provides with regard to transparency and safety of transactions.

#4: Reliability and longevity

The fact that Blockchain networks are decentralized means that they don't have a centralized point of failure. Therefore, in case one node fails in the network, the Blockchain network will still process the transaction, unlike centralized systems that rely on a single server.

#5: Process integrity

When you use the Blockchain technology, you can trust a transaction to be executed exactly as the protocol demands, without worrying about the need for a third party, because transactions are placed in the same block only if they have taken place at the same time. Other transactions, which are not yet in the same block, are considered to be unconfirmed.

Each miner can group transactions together into a block and broadcast the same information to all the network nodes as a recommendation for what the block should look like next, which improves the integrity of the system.

#6: Transparency and immutability

Any changes that are made to the public Blockchains are publicly accessible by all the nodes in the network. Thus, transparency is established. As a result of transparency, the transactions become immutable, meaning they cannot be changed or erased by other nodes.

So what now? Well, in the next subject matter, you will learn more about the finer details of transactions processing in the Blockchain technology. See you there.

Chapter 3

The Finer Details of Blockchain technology

Before we discuss the details of the Blockchain technology, it is important to have a big-picture understanding of transactions and how transactions are processed in Blockchain technology. I know we have mentioned the word transaction in several sections of this book. But what exactly is a transaction?

A transaction is a unit of work that is performed within the database management system against a database. The unit of work is always treated in a logical and reliable manner that is independent of other transactions. When a transaction occurs, we expect to have a change in database contents.

In the context of Blockchain technology, the transaction is handled within the program—the wallet—that carries out a series of steps, which results in a change of the database or the ledger. Now, for a transaction to take place, all of the steps must be completed or none of them at all. For instance, in Blockchain technology, all nodes must agree that the transaction has taken place.

At this point, I know you are eager to learn how transactions are processed in Blockchain technology. Let's jump in to find out.

How the transaction is processed

Blockchain transactions are usually sent from and to wallets—a piece of software installed on nodes—and digitally signed to enhance security. Every node on the network must be made aware of the transaction and the previous history of all the transactions. The transactions must be conducted in such a way that they can be traced back to the original Blockchain that was used.

For instance, if you wish to transact any business with your friend, then all you have to do is to broadcast a message to all the network nodes indicating that you wish to start the transaction. Each node in the Blockchain network will receive the broadcasted message and apply the requested transaction to their stored copy of the ledger.

Every transaction that ever takes place in the Blockchain ecosystem is stored in a ledger. The Blockchain is not stored on a central server or, if you are dealing with a centralized database system, then a single database server. On the other hand, if you are using the Blockchain technology, then ledger will be distributed among several nodes on the network. These nodes will be storing the data and executing the computations (transactions).

Each node in the Blockchain network receives the broadcasted message and applies the requested transaction to their stored copy of the ledger. Both of your wallet account details will be updated across all the nodes on the Blockchain network. The system uses a public key cryptography to encrypt and decrypt the broadcasted messages that are shared across the network.

The public key cryptography uses two keys to encrypt and decrypt the message: the private key and the public key. The public key—known to all the nodes—is used for encryption while the private key is used for decryption of the message. The private key is only known to the recipient of the message. It is also used to generate a digital signature, which authenticates the message being shared across the Blockchain network.

I know you're now thinking, "How does a transaction look like in Blockchain?"

A typical transaction has three components. These are:

- *The input.* An input is simply a record of the Blockchain address that was used to perform the transaction with the sender. Every time you reference the inputs in the transaction, those that are not considered valid will automatically reflect. This is done automatically in your wallet and it can be verified by any node in the Blockchain network.
- *The content of the transaction.* The content of the transaction is the actual transaction that you would like to perform on the network. If you are dealing with cryptocurrency system, then the content of the transaction will be the amount of money that you would like to exchange with the recipient.
- *The output.* The output is the recipient's Blockchain address.

So, how is the transaction initiated?

To initiate a transaction, you need to know the Blockchain address of the recipient and the private key. The address—a sequence of characters— will be produced randomly within the Blockchain network, while the private key—which is also a sequence of characters—is only known to the recipient.

I would like you to think of the address as some sort of a safe deposit box that has a glass front. Now every user knows what is contained in it. However, for you unlock the deposit box, you can only use the private key. The broadcast message is encoded with a particular public key, but it is only the owner of the paired private key who will be able to decrypt and read the contents of the message.

The recipient will now use his private key to decrypt the message. In other words, when you encrypt the broadcast message with your own private key, then it is only the paired public key that can be used to decrypt it. Every node in the network must cross check and validate that the transaction which has been requested is actually coming from you by decrypting the transacted broadcast message with the public key of your wallet.

So, whenever you're encrypting the transaction request with your own wallet's private key, what you are actually undertaking is generating a digital signature which will be used by Blockchain computers to verify and validate the source and the legitimacy of the transaction. The digital signature is simply a string of characters that combines your transaction request and your private key. It cannot be used for other transactions.

If you happen to change even a single character in the transaction, the digital signature will automatically change. This means that the transaction has been tampered with and all the nodes will be notified.

How fast are the Blockchain transactions?

Good question.

In a typical Blockchain transaction, you will have to wait for an average of 10 minutes for the transaction to be completed because every transaction that is initiated on the Blockchain network must be confirmed and authenticated by all the miners in the network. You will be forced to wait until all the miners have finished the confirmation and authentication processes.

The Blockchain network will check all the previous transactions that are related to your wallet using references that have inputs that point to your wallet account. All the records of unspent transactions will be stored by the Blockchain nodes. This simplifies the process of verification. As a result of this security check, it is nearly impossible to double- spend on a single transaction.

Of utmost importance to note in Blockchain technology is that the code that computes the transactions in the Blockchain is open source. This means that any person with a computer and an internet connection can initiate a transaction. If there is an error in the source code that broadcasts the transaction message, then all the associated transactions on the Blockchain will be forever lost.

Since the Blockchain system is distributed, there's no customer support in case you want to restore the transaction. That is why it is crucial to use only the recommended Blockchain wallet and store your password in a safe repository.

The Blockchain system arranges transactions by placing them together into groups which we call the blocks. Every block has a definite number of transactions. The transactions also link to the previous block, which forms a time-related chain.

The transactions can only be placed on the same block only if they have taken place at the same time. Other transactions that are not yet in the same block are considered unconfirmed. Each miner can group transactions together into a block and broadcast the same information to all the network nodes as a recommendation for what the block should look like next.

There you have it—all the Blockchain essentials that are necessary to get you started if you're interested in Blockchain technology. Now take this knowledge and determine whether you need Blockchain technology or not.

Performance metrics of the Blockchain technology

I know you're now asking, "How does Blockchain technology compare with centralized systems in terms of performance?"

Well, to compare the performance of the Blockchain technology with other technologies, we have to define performance metrics. Some of these metrics are:

- **Throughput.** Throughput refers to transactions executed in a unit of time. For instance, in Bitcoin cryptocurrency technology, a block is inserted in the chain only every 10 minutes (on average). Therefore, waiting for roughly 1 hour from when the transaction is added to the block for the first time will provide a high probability that the processed transaction is secure.
- **Scalability.** Scalability is a measure of the number of nodes that can be added to the network without affecting the performance of the Blockchain technology. Scalability is affected by the consensus of the algorithm used. For instance, using the proof of work algorithm may slow down the operation of the nodes if the nodes have low computational power. However, the proof of stake may still accommodate several nodes without affecting the throughput.
- **Stability.** Stability is the ability of the Blockchain network to remain operational even when some nodes in the network fail. It is a fact that Blockchain networks are fault tolerant because the ledger is distributed across several autonomous computers. Therefore, if one node fails, the rest of the nodes can still provide functionality.

- **Security.** Is Blockchain technology secure? Absolutely! Blockchain technology uses the public key cryptography to encrypt and decrypt transactions conducted across the network. Because different keys are used for encryption and decryption, it is almost impossible to hack into the Blockchain network.

Chapter 4

Consensus Mechanisms in Blockchain Technology

Dan O'Prey—the second co-founder of Hyperledger—had this to say about consensus mechanism:

"When you interact with multiple parties, you need some sort of consensus mechanism to ensure everyone has got the right records."

Building consensus is not a new idea. People have been building consensus since time immemorial. In its most definitive form, consensus allows different groups of people to reach an amicable decision without conflicts. For consensus to work there must be some sort of rules, regulations or even norms that must be acceptable to all members of the group.

Besides the rules, norms and regulations, all the members must have a sense of identity or ownership so that no one dictates his/her wishes to the rest of the group.

It is a fact that consensus began as a form of conflict resolution in societies. But now, it is a part and parcel of IT. In the last couple of years, a consensus has emerged as a solution to conflict among nodes that may arise in distributed systems. In distributed ledger systems, consensus helps a diverse set of autonomous nodes to make decisions that are devoid of conflict.

They also allow connected nodes to work harmoniously so that, even if one node fails in the network, the system still survives and provides normal functionality as if there was no network breakdown. In fact, it is correct to say that consensus mechanisms are the backbone of any Blockchain technology.

For instance, both the Bitcoin and the Ethereum cryptocurrency systems use a decentralized system that confirms transactions without relying on a trusted third party. Therefore, building consensus helps these diverse groups of autonomous computers make decisions that are devoid of conflict. In essence, the consensus mechanisms help the various nodes to agree on how transactions are updated in a coherent, logical, and immutable manner.

In fact, the consensus is the backbone of the Blockchain and any other distributed technologies.

Consensus mechanisms help a majority of autonomous computers to agree on the value of data or transaction that is entered on the Blockchain. This way, the connected autonomous computers work together as a group and the Blockchain network can still survive even if one of them has been hacked. The proof of work, proof of stake, and closed consensus are the most common algorithms used in Blockchain technologies.

So, how do consensus mechanisms work in Blockchain technology?

Let's dive in to find out how consensus mechanisms work in Blockchain technology.

Chapter 5

Factors to consider in consensus mechanisms

Before consensus mechanisms can be applied to a set of autonomous nodes in a Blockchain technology, they must fulfill certain parameters. Below are parameters that must be fulfilled before consensus mechanisms can be applied to a distributed set of autonomous computers in Blockchain technology:

- **Decentralized governance system.** This implies that a single node on the network can't determine the finality of the transaction. Besides the algorithm, all the nodes must have a sense of identity or ownership so that no node dictates his/her wishes to other autonomous computers in the Blockchain network.

- **Quorum structure.** The nodes must be structured in a manner that allows transacting in predefined ways. In Blockchain technology, the system arranges transactions by placing them together into groups, which we call the blocks. Every block has a definite number of transactions. The transactions also link to the previous block.
- **Authentication.** All the participating nodes must be identified in the system. In Blockchain system, authentication is achieved using digital signatures.
- *Integrity.* The validation of the transaction should remain intact. In other words, the output of the transaction should produce an immutable data in a transparent manner. In Blockchain system, authentication is achieved with digital signatures and the hashing function.
- **Non-repudiation.** Means must be provided to verify the initiator of the transaction. In Blockchain system, authentication is achieved using digital signatures and the hashing function.
- **Privacy.** Privacy helps to ensure that only the recipient is allowed to read the contents of the message. In other words, consensus mechanisms should guarantee that the communication is confidential. In Blockchain technology,

privacy is achieved by the public key cryptography system where the key used for encryption is different from the one used for decryption.
- **Fault tolerance.** The Blockchain network should continue to operate normally, even if some nodes have failed or slowed down. In fact, the connected autonomous computers should seamlessly work together as a single unit even if some of them have failed.
- **Performance.** The performance of the Blockchain system should be high. Even though several nodes have to agree for a transaction to be added to the Blockchain, this should not interfere with the throughput, scalability of the Blockchain system. While throughput refers to transactions that are being executed in a unit of time, scalability is the measure of the number of nodes that can be added to the network without affecting the performance of the Blockchain technology.

Now that you have understood what constitutes a good choice for selecting a consensus mechanism, let's jump in to find the different types, features, and demerits of consensus mechanisms.

#1: Proof of work

Proof of work is the most common consensus algorithm that is used in Blockchain technology. As the name suggests, the algorithm demands that decentralized nodes validate blocks by churning out enough random deductions. In this system, the sender of the message has to complete the proof of work algorithm so the receiving node would accept it.

Ideally, the miner builds a candidate block that is filled with transactions. Once the candidate block is established, the miner calculates the hash function—algorithm that determines the integrity of data—to determine if it can fit on the current target Blockchain. If the hash algorithm can't fit in the current Blockchain, it will automatically update the Blockchain by adding the transactions to it.

The main advantage of this consensus algorithm is that it provides miners with the financial incentive to process as many transactions as they want in shorter time. However, the downside of this application is that it can only be utilized in high throughput transaction systems because of the hash function that demands the correct update of the blocks.

Based on the hash function, the amount of work that must be performed is the exponential function of zero bits. This is the main pitfall of the protocol. As a result of this problem, the only method to get around it is by using the trial and error method so that we cannot guess the time it will take for the nodes to agree on adding a transaction.

However, in proof of work algorithm is accomplished by increasing the amount of computing power of the nodes. In other words, for the proof of work algorithm to work efficiently, all the nodes must meet basic hardware requirements, which include the clock speed and memory requirements.

#2: Proof of stake

The proof of stake algorithm is an alternative to proof of work algorithm. The main motivation of the algorithm allows the stakeholders in the network, who have the strongest inducements in adding the transactions to the Blockchain, to be good agents of the Blockchain system. In its simplest and purest form, the proof stake algorithm makes the process of mining easier for any node that can demonstrate control over the largest number of transactions.

For instance, in Bitcoin transactions, the proof of stake can start allowing the node that consumes so many bitcoins to have a pre-determined privilege in the network. Such a node can generate a block on itself, which will be agreed upon by all the nodes in the network. The initial block that is generated by the algorithm is referred to as the kernel. The kernel must meet the standards of the hash algorithm for the block to be accepted by other nodes.

Although the same hash function is applied to both the proof of work and proof of stake algorithm, the manner of applicability is different. For instance, in proof of stake algorithm, the computation is done in a limited search space, which makes it faster compared to the hash algorithm in proof of work, which works in unlimited search space.

In other words, every Blockchain transaction in the block must give its consuming work to the Blockchain. When several nodes with incentives take control of the consensus process, computing power is reduced in the hardware. Because of lack of computing power, the proof of stake algorithm eliminates the system from future hardware centralization.

Besides reducing the computational power, the proof of stake algorithm is difficult to be hacked because the kernel, which is initiated by the node with highest incentives, must meet the standards of the hash algorithm for the block to be accepted by other nodes. The transaction Validators are rewarded proportionately to the amount of incentive they own on the Blockchain network.

While, this approach improves the network security—discouraging simultaneous updates on the same block—it can only be enforced if the autonomous nodes have enough computational resources.

What are the pitfalls of this protocol?

Well, the proof of stake algorithm ensures that only the "richest" nodes— those with highest incentives—are the ones that take charge of the consensus process. This can create a problem of trust. Besides, the block generators may have nothing to lose when they vote for multiple Blockchain histories. This could lead to poor consensus in the Blockchain ecosystem.

#3: Closed consensus

In closed consensus algorithm, the nodes must place a "security deposit" to update given blocks on the Blockchain. The presence of the security deposits in the system incentivizes the validators to update blocks on the Blockchain. In case there are disagreements on some blocks, the "arbitrators" are created to help solve the conflict.

Essentially, the arbitrators are the conflict management nodes that take the responsibility to resolve errors and conflicts, which may occur during the update of blocks by nodes with security deposits. So, how are arbitrators selected? The arbitrators are selected based on the protocol that is commonly known as GHOST (Greedy Heaviest Observed Sub Tree).

The main function of the GHOST protocol is to enforce consensus across all the nodes in the Blockchain network. In case, there are disagreements, the validator must authenticate the transaction, which the GHOST protocol has considered legitimate. If this is the case, the validator must lose its security deposits. Furthermore, such validators will also forfeit their Blockchain privileges of providing consensus in the Blockchain network.

#4: Federated Byzantine Agreement (FBA)

The Federated Byzantine Agreement consensus algorithm assumes that all the nodes in the Blockchain know all other participants. Besides knowing other participants, they should be able to distinguish those nodes with higher incentives in the Blockchain ecosystem. If a node wishes to update a given block on the Blockchain, it must wait for the majority of other miners in the system to agree to the transaction.

Once all the other nodes have agreed, the transaction is regarded settled and the related block is updated on the Blockchain. But nodes with highest incentives on the network cannot agree on the transaction until all the other participants have agreed. This means that, for a given block to be updated on the Blockchain, both the normal and important nodes in the network must agree with each other.

In a nutshell, the Federated Byzantine algorithm relies on a very small set of trusted parties—the nodes with the highest incentives. These nodes trust each other's data. When enough of these trusted nodes have been formed, the other nodes in the system will always reach a consensus based on the assumption that trusted nodes have agreed.

#5: Byzantine Fault Tolerant

Distributed ledger systems can use the Byzantine Fault Tolerant consensus algorithm as a way to allow nodes in the Blockchain network to reach consensus. In this protocol, each miner publishes its public key (remember, Blockchain system is based on public key cryptography). Now, data that is coming through the miner must be signed to verify its format. If enough similar responses have been reached, the data being transmitted is regarded to be a valid transaction.

This protocol requires systems that have low latency storage. These systems have very low throughput and have many transactions to be updated. The main objective of this algorithm is to reach consensus in a faster and efficient manner. Nevertheless, for the protocol to work, trust must be decoupled from the resource ownership so it becomes possible for nodes with the lowest incentives to participate in the consensus process.

Now you know why consensus mechanisms are important in Blockchain technology and the different algorithms that are used in Blockchain ecosystem.

Chapter 6

Challenges of the Blockchain Technology

In this chapter, we explore the pros and cons of the Blockchain technology, difficulties of the Blockchain systems and the security of the Blockchain system. By the end of the chapter, you will have a broader picture of how Blockchain technology can help your organization. Let's dive in.

Pros of the Blockchain technology

Below are some of the advantages of the Blockchain technology:

#1: Transparency and immutability

Information is transparent. All the processed transactions are available for any node to view even though the personal information is usually hidden. In fact, the public address is what is visible to everyone but the personal data is not tied to the public address. Any changes that are made to the public Blockchains are publicly accessible by all the nodes in the network.

Thus, transparency is established. As a result of transparency, the transactions become immutable, meaning they cannot be changed or erased by other nodes.

#2: It establishes the reliability and the longevity of data

The fact that Blockchain networks are decentralized means that they don't have a centralized point of failure. Therefore, in case one node fails in the network, the Blockchain network will still process transactions, unlike centralized systems that rely on a single server. This promotes reliability of data that is stored on the Blockchain network.

On the other hand, the immutability of data ensures that all transactions are kept in the Blockchain for a very long period where every node can inspect them at any point in time.

#3: Trust

The main reason why Blockchain technology is superior to centralized database management systems is that it provides user's trust in the global-wide decentralized and open source system. The fact that there's low probability of solving the blocks simultaneously makes the system trustworthy.

In essence, it prevents transactions on multiple blocks in a repeated fashion. In fact, transactions will get more and more secure as time elapses. Transactions included in the blocks confirmed in the past are regarded more secure than blocks included in the recent block. As a result of this feature, this system guarantees trusted communication among the Blockchain nodes.

#4: It promotes innovation

With other cryptocurrency systems such as Ethereum and Litecoin invented on the Blockchain, there are always developers keen to improve on the existing protocol. In fact, if the centralized networks were part of the privatized Blockchains, that would provide serious thoughts on how to make them robust and transparent because of the synergy that's created by two technologies. Essentially, private Blockchains will open all avenues for fresh ideas and innovation. You can think of the conventional database system as an "intranet." Now, the intranet on its own cannot allow you to revolutionize and bring in fresh innovative ideas to your company.

Nevertheless, when you combine the intranet and the internet, which is what the Blockchain technology is providing, you have a perfect mix of innovation and external options with massive amounts of control to your organization. In other words, you will be in a position to leverage the Blockchain technology to create other decentralized applications that are able to manage data efficiently and transfer value in a secure manner.

#5: It allows a user to gain complete control of all the transactions

If you apply the Blockchain technology in implementing the cryptocurrency systems, you will gain complete control over the transactions. Imagine a scenario where you have cash and you would like to spend it without involving a third party. In this scenario, you are not bothered about the bank charges and other levied charges when transacting goods and services.

Again, there will be no forms in case you want to give your cryptocurrency money to someone else. This is what you get with a Blockchain technology. When the technology is cascaded to other applications, such as smart contracts, you will begin to appreciate the level of control that it provides with regard to transparency and safety of transactions.

#6: It ensures integrity of transactions

The validation of the transaction remains intact. In other words, when you use the Blockchain technology, using digital signatures and the hashing function, the output of the transaction will always produce transparent and immutable data.

Cons of the Blockchain technology

Below are disadvantages of the Blockchain technology:

#1: The technology is still in infancy stage

The Blockchain technology is still at an infancy stage. Therefore, the implementation of the Therefore, the implementation of Blockchain technology in organizations might still pose a major challenge with regard to the transaction speed, the verification of transactions, and data limits.

#2: Uncertainties in the regulatory status of the Blockchain technology

The application of Blockchain technology in cryptocurrency system such as Bitcoin and Ethereum has presented governments with unprecedented challenges of regulation. National governments regulate modern conventional currencies, while the Blockchain technology remains unregulated.

Because of the unregulated nature of the Blockchain technology, its adoption is still low in financial institutions.

#3: It requires enormous computational resources

The Blockchain network users usually attempt a thousand trillions of transactions per second, which requires enormous computational resources in terms of hardware. For instance, the proof of work algorithm, which is the most popular consensus algorithm, is used in cryptocurrency systems. In it, all the nodes must meet basic hardware requirements, which include the clock speed and memory requirements.

#4: Security and privacy challenges still exists

While the Blockchain technology has ensured there is a full-proof cryptographic security protocol, there are still some security concerns that have to be addressed before the public can have confidence in the application system in various domains.

#5: Persistent Integration concerns

The Blockchain applications provide solutions, which demand significant changes to the system. For instance, complete replacement of existing information system may be required for implementation of the Blockchain technology. Therefore, switching to Blockchain technology requires strategies, which organizations may lack.

#6: Cyber attacks

Hackers can use Blockchain cryptographic algorithms for malicious activities without leaving traces. In fact, cryptographic systems are widely used on the dark web in the trade of illegal services, beyond government regulations and consent. It is true that the use of bitcoins has fueled frauds and thefts, which have infuriated the global financial institutions and government agencies.

#7: Irreversibility

Any data encrypted in the cryptographic Blockchain network may not be accessible if the true user forgets or even loses his/her private keys.

Next, let's review some of the difficulties in adopting the Blockchain technology in an organization.

The difficulties of adopting Blockchain technology

Let's be honest—the Blockchain technology has had an exponential impact on the financial, health, elections and asset management. Nevertheless, organizations are finding it difficult to adopt the system in providing cost-effective solutions to their problems. For instance, in cryptocurrency systems, most banks find it difficult to adopt the system despite its massive benefits in terms of providing transparent, secure and cost-effective solutions to the banking problems.

So, what are the difficulties in adopting the Blockchain technology?

Below are the main problems with regard to the adoption of Blockchain technology:

#1: Most institutions are still making profits with centralized systems

It is a fact that most banks are still making huge profits on their financial transactions with the centralized systems. It is a fact that most financial institutions still want to exert control in the way currencies are stored and exchanged—something that the Blockchain technology strives to eliminate.

In addition, most financial organizations have invested in massive infrastructure that supports centralized system of banking. Therefore, convincing them to switch to Blockchain technology is a herculean task. In fact, trying to overhaul the whole banking infrastructure is a tall order and poses a huge risk, which is something that most organizations are unwilling to undertake.

#2: Priorities

Most firms are in dilemma on what to do in a fast-paced, complex and ever-evolving business environment dictated by the exponential growth of the internet. For instance, most financial institutions are already having a huge technological nightmare—keeping abreast with internet competition and regulation. Therefore, there are very high stakes, which keep on shifting. This makes it extremely difficult to justify investments in the Blockchain technology.

#3: Majority of organizations still use bureaucratic systems

Rethinking and re-engineering an organization requires more than just a collection of ideas and incubators. This is true if the organization is still bureaucratic. Frankly, most firms haven't been wired to drive such kind of disruptive innovation in their organization. For instance, lawyers, accountant ants, front office staff, etc. will always have different opposing views, which may make it extremely difficult to adopt the idea of Blockchain implementation in an organization.

Just imagine approaching all these stakeholders in the organization to convince them to adopt the Blockchain technology! Besides that, add this caveat; the technology could overturn the key fundamentals of the organization that threatens its existence. It is simply not easy to sell that idea.

Chapter 7

The Future of Blockchain Technology

The initial application of the Blockchain technology, usually dubbed Blockchain 1.0, was in Bitcoin cryptocurrency systems. The goal of the Bitcoin cryptocurrency system was to replace the fiat money. As the technology grew, it entered another era, commonly referred to as Blockchain 2.0. Blockchain 2.0 is based on digital assets and smart property management.

Digital assets are those assets where an ownership is recorded in electronic form. For instance, the bitcoins are examples of digital assets. However, since the Blockchain is a decentralized system of asset registry, it can be used to register the ownership and transfer of digital assets. The shift in the expansion of Blockchain application happened around the year 2013/2014. However, the process is still ongoing.

In summary, the application of the Blockchain technology can be viewed from the following four perspectives:

- Cryptocurrency systems
- Value registry systems
- Value ecosystems
- Value web form systems

Let's jump to the applications of the Blockchain network.

#1: Cryptocurrency systems

A cryptocurrency system—sometimes called virtual currency—is new unregulated digital money, unlike the conventional currency such as the US Dollars, the Euro, and the sterling pounds that you normally use. A community of Blockchain developers manages and controls these currencies. For to you use a cryptocurrency, you have to subscribe to it and gain membership into that virtual currency community.

In other words, the cryptocurrency system is just like the normal cash system (money in coins and notes) that you can access at any point in time without having to worry about the bank charges and other charges that banks levy. With the cryptocurrency, you will not have to worry about bank charges, currency conversion rates, or filling out forms every time you want to send money to a friend.

Why are cryptocurrency systems gaining attention from several financial and technology firms?

Good question.

The exponential growth of the Internet has completely altered how people buy and sell goods and services. With inordinate online marketplaces such as the eBay, the Amazon, and other storefronts, all you have to do to buy a given product is simply to research the product you want to buy from the comfort of your home. Once you have settled on the right product, you will use your credit card to complete the purchasing process.

Concisely, the internet has completely changed how commerce is conducted. People are no longer buying from the brick and mortar shops. Online marketplaces have continued to grow because of the internet. However, the intricacies that usually accompany online buying with regard to online payment systems such as PayPal and Skrill are just many. For you to use these online payment systems, you must have an e-mail address and valid bank credit/debit card.

In some cases, these services might freeze your account without any warnings. In addition, there are high transaction costs that you are forced to pay. Because of these challenges, most users prefer to use the cryptocurrency systems. Cryptocurrencies resembles cash. Instead of buying goods and services from the brick and mortar shops using the cash, you'll be using the cryptocurrencies to buy goods and services from online marketplaces.

Ever since its invention, the media has been extensively covering the Bitcoin system in the news. The natural consequence of its increasing recognition has been the ability to provide an open source currency that allows everyone to apply for it and use it without the consensus of any authority.

Some of the advantages of the Bitcoin cryptocurrency system:

- They are transparent. Information is transparent. All the processed transactions are available for any node to view even though the personal information is usually hidden.
- They guarantee reliability and longevity of data. The fact that they use the Blockchain technology means that they do not have a centralized point of failure.
- They establish trust in the use of the currency. The transactions conducted on the network are almost impossible to hack because of strong cryptographic mechanisms.

- They ensure the integrity of transactions. The validation of the transaction, achieved with digital signatures and the hashing function, remains intact.

#2: Value registry systems

Think of high-valued properties as assets such as the real estate, land, cars, and even art. Now, for any high-valued properties, it is critical that their accurate records are maintained. In the case of land management, it is vital to have a system that allows land administrators to record, track, and transfer deeds in a transparent, cost-effective and incorruptible manner.

Conventional registry management systems rely on trusted third systems—such as government agencies or witnesses— to verify and keep track of the ownership data. This opens the system to fraud in areas where the data is not stored systematically. However, the implementation of the Blockchain system can eliminate fraud in the management of such properties.

If the Blockchain technology is used, it can help financial institutions, mortgage companies, to help reduce the time it takes to search the deeds in a transparent manner. This technology can help in the management of these high-valued properties to easily identify the current owner and provide proof that he/she is indeed the owner of that particular property.

The ability to prove that a property belongs to an individual is the central objective that underpins the Blockchain technology in the management of value registry systems. So, how can the Blockchain prove that an individual owns a property? Well, at the minimum, the Blockchain technology uses consensus algorithms such as proof of work or proof of stake to keep track and manage how changes in the transactions will be handled.

Therefore, a transaction can only be updated on the Blockchain if all the nodes in the network have agreed. By using consensus algorithms, this system will eliminate fraud. The following is a summary of how the consensus algorithm will resolve the problem of double allocation of property to different individuals:

At some given point in time, the property (land, cars, real estate, or art) will be associated with a certain transaction output, which forms the genesis of the transaction output. This transaction output belongs to the initial owner.

If the property happens to be sold or transferred to another person, the system will find the transaction output, which already belongs to the previous owner, and provides information how it has been spent. At this point, the transaction is updated on the Blockchain. However, remember that all the nodes in the system must receive notifications of the purchase or the transfer so that they can update their blocks. However, for them to update the ledger, they have to use either proof of work or proof of stake algorithms. Once they have agreed, the output is transferred to the owner and the Blockchain is updated.

If someone wants to identify the owner, the miner will search through the transaction history starting from the initial transaction or genesis transaction up to the current/unspent transaction output. This is how the Blockchain network can provide proof of ownership of property.

#3: Value ecosystems

Until now, we have focused on the expansion of the Blockchain from Blockchain 1.0 to 2.0. This development has made the technology more efficient and applicable than it is when it is just used as a currency. Up to this point, it's important to note that all the protocols presented are specialized. This means that they provide specific and targeted features to users.

For instance, when the Blockchain technology is used in land management, the system is being targeted in value registry management. On the same note, the Bitcoin network, which relies on Blockchain, provides cryptocurrency solutions in the financial technology industry.

However, the Blockchain technology has been expanding at the exponential rate, not just fast but really fast! In the midst of the growth, there are communities of developers that have taken an opposite approach. This approach entails creating a Blockchain system that is as general as possible. These systems allow any user to create and serve any specialized purpose based on the Blockchain application.

These developers have been creating building blocks, which allow users to develop systems that can be utilized in a variety of applications. The two examples of value ecosystems are the Ethereum and smart contracts. Let's find out how these two examples of Blockchain differ.

#1: Ethereum

The Ethereum network is a virtual currency, just like the bitcoin. It can be regarded as a private Blockchain network solution that can act as global fabric for finance. Both the Bitcoin and the Ethereum have one main objective: to create an open-source currency system that allows any person to use them without any regulations. But there are some differences between the Ethereum and Bitcoin systems that are three-fold.

First, the Ethereum system uses the turning complete as a programming language while the Bitcoin system is based on the stack-based language. The use of turning complete programming language ensures that the virtual currency executes in the same manner without being hacked and without presenting downtime hitches. On the other hand, the stack-based programming language ensures that transactions are valid.

Second, the Ethereum currency system is faster compared to the Bitcoin. In fact, the transaction time or throughput in Ethereum is twelve seconds while in Bitcoin the throughput is 10 minutes.

Finally, the Ethereum system doesn't provide any economic rewards after 4 years. However, in the Bitcoin network, the economic returns are usually halved after every 4 years. All the same, when it comes to the reserve side matters of the digital currency, there's no limit in Ethereum.

#2: Smart contracts

Smart contracts can be regarded as the next generation Blockchain technologies that are implemented using the Blockchain 2.0 platform. The smart contracts have the capability to manage any enterprise system. Generally speaking, the smart contracts can be regarded as autonomous computer system programs—written in some programming language—that manage the contracts between users on the Blockchain ecosystem.

The programming codes reside at specific addresses on any of the Ethereum Blockchain system. This system is commonly known as the Ethereum Virtual Machine (EVM) bytecode. Because the Ethereum virtual machine manages contracts between autonomous nodes, they can pass messages among themselves using very complex complete computational algorithms. Smart contracts can be developed using programming languages such as the Solidity, Serpent, and LLL.

#4: Value web form systems

It is not a secret that the Blockchain technology hinged around the trading of financial assets and became successful in transaction banking and payment systems in organizations. The value web—also called the "internet of value"—is the next massive evolution of the Blockchain technology that is expected to emerge from a combination of different internet technologies where Blockchain is the main pillar.

Of course, we are not there yet. Nevertheless, the world of finance is set to undergo a disruptive revolution when several internet technologies merge with the Blockchain technology. One benefit that will arise from the Blockchain technology will be the speed at which transactions are processed in the Blockchain technology.

Currently, the Ethereum takes 12 seconds to process a single transaction while Bitcoin takes an average of 10 minutes. With the introduction of Value web forms, the throughputs are set to increase. Therefore, the existing financial services could be powered by the Blockchain systems at lower costs in a shorter time.

Well, that's it. What's your take on the future of out the Blockchain technology? Next, we will review the legal implications of the Blockchain technology

Chapter 8

Legal Implications of Blockchain Technology

No other technology, apart from Blockchain technology, has disrupted businesses since the invention of the internet. As a demonstration of the power of the Blockchain technology, several financial institutions have shown interest in investing in this distributed ledger system technology. Some have actually adopted the system and are beginning to reap its benefits.

Despite the massive benefits of the technology, most organizations are yet fully to understand the concept of the distributed ledgers, let alone their real utilities when they are invested in the organization. Since the invention of the internet only one buzzword—the Blockchain—has caused so much hype.

One area where technology is creating confusion is in governments and provisions of regulatory frameworks for its adoption and use. In fact, most companies and governments are finding it difficult to formulate rules and regulations that govern the use of the Blockchain technology.

It is clear that the Blockchain technology has significant capacities to transform a variety of industries and organization. That, however, is not a panacea for wholesome adoption without questioning its legal implications. Just as it is the case with any disruptive technology, the Blockchain technology raises a number of queries for any policy-making institution and regulator.

These institutions may operate at national or international levels. Because of the complex nature of the technology—which relies on the internet—most regulators are cautiously taking the "wait and see" approach when it comes to formulating laws, rules, and framework that guides its application.

The Blockchain technology isn't without its fair share of challenges that includes scalability, latency, lack of understanding, inadequate readiness in some organizations, and over-relying on the legacy and conventional systems. Of utmost importance is the fact that successful adoption of the Blockchain technology requires collaboration across all interested stakeholders. When I say stakeholders, I allude to even the regulators who formulate laws and policies on the Blockchain usage.

For instance, in the financial industry, the market traders and their advisors should work with other trading firms, exchange system, clearing and settlement institutions, trade organization bodies and regulators to develop standardization and interoperability concerns before the Blockchain network can be rolled out. In most cases, this is easier said than done.

From a legal and regulatory viewpoint, any system that creates or adopts the Blockchain technology must resemble any large-scale negotiation and implementation of an IT project. The implementation of Blockchain technology will pose serious legal and regulatory challenges. Let's dive in to find out these legal implications of implementing the Blockchain technology.

Chapter 9

Legal impacts of the Blockchain technology

Below are legal implications of implementing the Blockchain technology in an organization:

#1: Accountability/responsibility

One of the main challenges that are likely to arise in the use of Blockchain technology is accountability. Who will be accountable for transactions that are updated on the Blockchain? Now, control over the Blockchain system is usually distributed to several autonomous nodes. Remember that the Blockchain system only shares the public address. However, the public address does not mask the identity of a node.

So, how can you control or regulate the Blockchain? More fundamentally, the question is who will be accountable in that distributed and decentralized system; whose and what data will you regulate. These are burning queries that present themselves whenever any firm implements the Blockchain system. In most cases, it will be likely that some sorts of international regulatory principles are put in place. But these measures alone can't answer the basic queries raised with regard to accountability and responsibility unless there's cooperation among the national regulators.

#2: Smart contract laws

Smart contracts can be regarded as autonomous computer system programs—written in some programming language—that manage the contracts between users on the Blockchain ecosystem. In a normal system, the law manages those contracts. An agreement can be said to have taken place when it is enforceable by relevant laws of a country or by the international law.

Ideally, the basic tenets of any contract are the mutual assent, the consideration, the capacity, and the legality. Now, how is a smart contract going to be enforced by relevant laws of a country? Will it be lawful and enforceable? In most cases, countries have not implemented laws that regulate the smart contracts.

#3: Privacy and security

The Blockchain technology relies on the assumption that it is secure, based on the cryptographic protocols used. Truth to be told—it is very difficult to hack a Blockchain system. However, that does not mean it is impossible. With the continued development of the quantum computing—which will result in faster computers—it may not be the case. Other security concerns may arise. For example, in the future, it might be possible to trace the node's identity from the Blockchain transactions or even through a node that has the permissions to decrypt the data.

#4: Competition/anti-trust

If the private Blockchains are created that are the same as consortia, then there could be arguments of cartel activities in the ecosystem. In addition, this could indicate a risk that the algorithms have produced anti-competitive results, which are secretive and hardly detectable.

CONCLUSION

Those institutions—whether in financial or technology sectors—that are willing to move first are most likely going to gain the largest benefits from the Blockchain technology. In the recent past, several companies have raced to leverage Blockchain technology in order to develop new products and services.

I know that the Blockchain technology is still at its infancy stage. It is an emerging area of innovation, which is not coming from a vacuum. There are reasons why several centralized systems aren't working. Problems of transparency, trust, security, and openness are making users think differently about the management of assets, currency systems, and contracts.

It is a fact that the impact of Blockchain on various industries will very much depend on the cooperation and its adoption in organizations. You should be a part of the team that uses Blockchain technology to grow your organization.

Even though the Blockchain technology doesn't provide the picture-perfect technology right out of the gates, you should also note that neither the mobile phone nor the Internet were perfect at first launch. All these technologies had their fair share of challenges when they were first introduced.

Nevertheless, the Blockchain technology provides a perfect incentive for business process changes in organizations. This type of prospect doesn't present itself that regularly. What am I trying to say? Embrace the idea of openness, decentralization, distribution and speed that the Blockchain network provides. Exactly these characteristics drew users to the Bitcoin network.

Did you like this book? Would you like to read more of such great book like this one? Then, why not subscribe to our website and receive free books notification (limited time) on similar topics?

ABOUT THE AUTHOR

Victor Finch is a zealous enthusiast for the latest technology, innovative gadgets and financial subjects ranging from Fintech to stock trading. These interests strike a deep resonating chord in his passions. He is an entrepreneur, an IT consultant, and a part-time author.

Victor as a child was always fascinated with how things worked; breaking apart his childhood toys is a common sight. Victor always has some innovative workarounds or solutions for his friends or family's problems such as a stubborn laptop that just like to "sleep" and how to improve the quality of life for his family.

If you spot someone, penning down his thoughts while walking down the streets of New York. That could be our dear Victor. He is always intrigued by the latest creativities around and just wants to tinkle with them when he has some me time.

In his spare time, Victor likes to explore the world, read his favorite books, open his little notes and write his next best seller book.

Did you like this book?

If you would like to read more great books like this one, why not subscribe to our website and receive <u>LIFETIME Updates</u> on all our latest promotions, upcoming books and new book releases, and free books or gifts that we occasionally pamper our loyal members.

http://goo.gl/b8Au77

Check out Victor's other proud works below if you didn't get a chance or follow Victor at

https://goo.gl/y0TVE3

Thanks for reading! Please add a short review on Amazon and let me know what your thoughts! - Victor

- END -

technic
2y

Ticketnr. NYEGOSWQIB

Made in the USA
Middletown, DE
22 February 2017